Baryshnikov at Work

Baryshnikov at Work

MIKHAIL BARYSHNIKOV DISCUSSES HIS ROLES

PHOTOGRAPHS BY MARTHA SWOPE
TEXT EDITED AND INTRODUCED BY
CHARLES ENGELL FRANCE

ALFRED A. KNOPF ⟩⟨ NEW YORK, 1983

THIS IS A BORZOI BOOK PUBLISHED BY ALFRED A. KNOPF, INC.
Text Copyright © 1976 by Mikhail Baryshnikov
Photographs Copyright © 1974, 1975, 1976 by Martha Swope
Introduction Copyright © 1976 by Charles Engell France
All rights reserved under International and Pan-American Copyright Conventions.
Published in the United States by Alfred A. Knopf, Inc., New York, and simultaneously
in Canada by Random House of Canada Limited, Toronto.
Distributed by Random House, Inc., New York.
Library of Congress Cataloging in Publication Data
Baryshnikov, Mikhail, [date]
Baryshnikov at work.
1. Baryshnikov, Mikhail, [date]   2. Dancers — Biography.
I. Swope, Martha.   II. France, Charles Engell.   III. Title.
GV1785.B348A33   1978   792.8' 092' 4   [B]   76-13685
ISBN 0-394-40345-2   ISBN 0-394-73587-0 pbk.
Manufactured in the United States of America
Published December 16, 1976
Reprinted Once
Third Printing, September 1979
First Paperback Edition February 1978
Reprinted Four Times
Sixth Paperback Printing, November 1983

GRAPHIC CREDITS
GRAPHIC DIRECTOR: R. D. SCUDELLARI
SPENCERIAN TITLES: GUN LARSON
PRODUCTION DIRECTOR: ELLEN McNEILLY
COMPOSITOR: QUAD TYPOGRAPHERS
PRINTER: RAPOPORT PRINTING CORPORATION
BINDER: AMERICAN BOOK — STRATFORD PRESS

CONTENTS

INTRODUCTION BY CHARLES ENGELL FRANCE

This was not an easy book to make…Mikhail Baryshnikov is a very modest man. But fortunately his life is his work. And on the subject of his work he is passionate and expansive. Since he began to dance in the West, Baryshnikov has attacked his work with a vengeance, dancing more than twenty new roles in less than two years. This book is a history in pictures of that period and a history in words of how he felt about every role he danced — what it was like to perform new works in styles he had never dreamed of attempting, what it was like to develop the ones he knew. Perhaps never before has an artist of such impact and importance taken the time in the middle of such an extraordinarily active career to document his *development,* his artistic curiosity, and the sheer work of it all.

We began to make this book in September of 1975. Discarding the notion of writing a book in Russian and having it translated, Baryshnikov, whose English was already impressive — and expressive — began to "speak" his thoughts: mostly in English, although he did often speak in Russian, which was translated for me. It was my job to take down what he said, organize it, and then often encourage him to overcome a certain reticence and expand on his subject. We would then work together until he was satisfied. Baryshnikov is just at the beginning of a new life, a man driven to explore as many aspects of his art as possible — all with a dedication and concentration that are consuming. No one can easily capture his zeal and his energy, and it is impossible to stress enough the astonishing care and preparation he gives to every role. Although basically an instinctive and spontaneous performer, he devotes hours to every aspect of every work — its history, its music, its technique, its poetic life. A great deal of that preparation, of course, cannot be recorded; besides, the whole book was always thought of in the light of a statement Baryshnikov made the day we began: "I don't want to make *pronouncements.* Who am I to speak that way — I'm still in the middle of everything. I can just try to say what I feel now. Who knows what I'll think of all these things in five or ten years?" And yet, for all his diffidence, it seems to me that in this book he reveals himself as an artist to an exceptional degree.

Martha Swope, whose beautiful photographs grace this book, was able to take performance shots of every ballet Baryshnikov has danced since he came to the West with the exception of a short piece that was danced once only in Hamburg (and which was photographed later). Martha spent hundreds of hours taking and printing the pictures, as well as traveling to England and Canada to ensure a complete record — her trials and tribulations in getting the pictures could make an entire book. In addition, Baryshnikov was persuaded to work occasionally with Martha in the studio at times when we all felt — as with *Petrouchka* — that something special could be gained from its more controlled and focused environment.

Robert Scudellari designed this book as a labor of love, making and remaking layouts and working tirelessly with Martha to achieve the most sensitive photographic reflection of the variety and scope of Baryshnikov's art.

Robert Gottlieb of Knopf, *maestro extra-ordinaire,* orchestrated all this activity with his special élan and an enviable sense of cool. The original idea of the book was his, and at the end it was he who convinced us all to work through the summer of 1976 (against frightening production deadlines) because Baryshnikov had several new and important roles to dance for the first time, including *Petrouchka* and *The Sleeping Beauty.*

Finally, there is one other person without whom the whole project would have been doomed. Remi Saunder, who in the early months acted as Baryshnikov's interpreter — and always as his friend — devoted as much time to the book as any of us, with her unfailing zest, her unquenchable good humor, and her heightened appreciation of the realities involved…a very special lady indeed.

This book must be called a collaboration in the highest sense of the word. We all worked together with a special harmony and serenity that sprang both from mutual affection and a mutual goal: to capture an extraordinary period in an extraordinary dancer's life; to display Baryshnikov's range, to reveal his passion for his work. Baryshnikov has many years to dance and many more roles to assume, but no time will ever be as this one was. To have shared it with him has been a privilege.

WORKING: A PREFACE BY MIKHAIL BARYSHNIKOV

It was with Alexander Pushkin that I began the final stages of my work to become a dancer. I had begun my training in Riga, Latvia, where I was born, and had studied for four years in the State Ballet Academy there before transferring to the Kirov School in Leningrad. It was then, at fifteen, that I became a student of Pushkin, and it was during the years I studied with this extraordinary man that my basic ideas on dancing and work took shape. Everything he gave me is in one way or another the beginning — the solid beginning — of how I now understand it all.

Pushkin was, of course, the most famous teacher of classical male dancers in Russia, the last in a line of gifted ballet pedagogues that goes back to the nineteenth century. He trained and perfected the technique and style of thousands of male students, and his pupils were to be found as the leading dancers in all the Soviet Republics. His achievements are perhaps unparalleled in the history of Soviet ballet.

Pushkin's influence was enormous. His experience in the classroom was unmatched, and his authority unquestionable. A calm, serene man, he was not given to elaborate verbal instructions. His style was the simplest — quiet and direct, but never confining. He very often began by helping a dancer choose a line to pursue. That is, early on in his students' careers he would steer them in one direction or another: this one toward the romantic-lyrical route, that one toward the virtuoso. He taught in such a way that the dancer began to know himself more completely, and that, I believe, is the first key to serious work, to becoming an artist — to know oneself, one's gifts, one's limitations, as fully as possible. It is the only way. Any dancer will always be his own sternest critic, but real work means knowing how to invest the time, first to see yourself clearly for what you are, and then to recognize what you might become. Pushkin had this ability — to guide the dancer down the right path toward being realistic about his gifts, and then to inspire him to work, and work hard, at making the most artistically of those gifts. He also taught me that no one else can assume this responsibility — an invaluable lesson. He didn't force you, he gave his wisdom freely, and you did with it what you could and would.

Pushkin's greatest gift to me was in stagecraft. He taught me about the difference between technique — dancing in the classroom — and *real* dancing. Real dancing happens on the space of a stage, and to be aware of that space — its flexibility, its rules, its relationship to the audience—was what he stressed. As I work now, I still am always aware of those early lessons. One goes out onstage with a well-prepared technique, a knowledge of how to present that technique in its most refined form. But beyond that, what counts is the ability to be free on the stage, to *dance.* When I prepare a role, I naturally learn the steps first; however, I try to find the appropriate style from the beginning, and then rehearse the steps in it. As a young dancer I had a quite developed, secure technique, but my sense of style was often appalling. I now know that style is what gives blood and color to the bones of the piece, the technique. It is of the utmost importance to work very hard to make technique and style one. The *sauts de basque* of *Don Quixote, Coppélia,* and *Flames of Paris* are all basically the same step, but the styles are quite different: the first sharp and playfully arrogant, the second purely pure, the last broadly heroic. In other words, the performance of any given step onstage should never be merely a technical exposition, however perfect. Classical technique is like any language: it can be correctly spoken in many voices.

It takes time and work to execute the classroom step in any given style, to make it natural, make it seamlessly connected, so that it is true, honest, when performed. I work very hard at that. Of course, I also work to maintain the most harmonious and developed technique I possibly can. This means class every day and then attention, always attention, to specific problems. Every dancer has weak spots. I work, for example, to lengthen the line of the body, to give breadth to all the movement, to present my body honestly but at its best—for example, in certain jumps, to hold the movement in the air one second longer so that the movement suggests the potential for yet a further bit of stretch. The line mustn't be squared off. Thus the illusion of further lengthening the line in the air is created.

When I'm working on a new role, I commit myself one hundred percent; it's the only way—to have complete faith. *Later* you can be critical. As I said, first the steps, always with a certain knowledge of how and why; I rarely can or do proceed without some idea of what I'm doing. Tudor's *Shadowplay* was a rare exception, when I learned the role without "knowing." It was a rare lesson too, when I found out what it was all about.

I have been very lucky to work in so many new ballets, but to me that is what a dancer's work is — to have as large a variety of challenges as possible. Every ballet, whether or not successful artistically and with the public, has given me something important I could store up for future use, just as when I studied character dancing as a student, it gave me a certain sense of freedom even in the classical roles. Well, everything that I've done has given me more freedom. Imagine — to have danced for the first time ballets by Robbins and Balanchine and Tudor and Twyla Tharp, and Fokine's *Petrouchka,* and Alvin Ailey — all of them. It's like learning many, many new languages, all of which expand one's flexibility and range. The dancer, just like the language scholar, needs as many as possible. There are never enough.

In developing a new role, then, I begin with the steps and the style. If it is a dramatic part, I don't act it out. I think about it all the time…in rehearsal and outside. But I try to keep it fresh for the stage. If you get it all in rehearsal, it so easily becomes cold and stale. And that's a trap.

And last and first is the music. Musicality is not completely an instinct. It too is like dancing, a combination of technical education and sense of style, of understanding what the emotional and dramatic intent of the music is. Any music that I dance I listen to over and over until it becomes part of me. I don't listen to it in terms of what I am going to dance, but to learn its own life, its own shape.

As a teenager I knew that whatever I was to become I wanted to be very good at. So a decision had to be made. I decided to be a dancer, and I still work at becoming very good. Working is living to me. Nobody is *born* a dancer; you have to want it more than anything. That desire is the discipline of a career, and work is the language of that discipline.

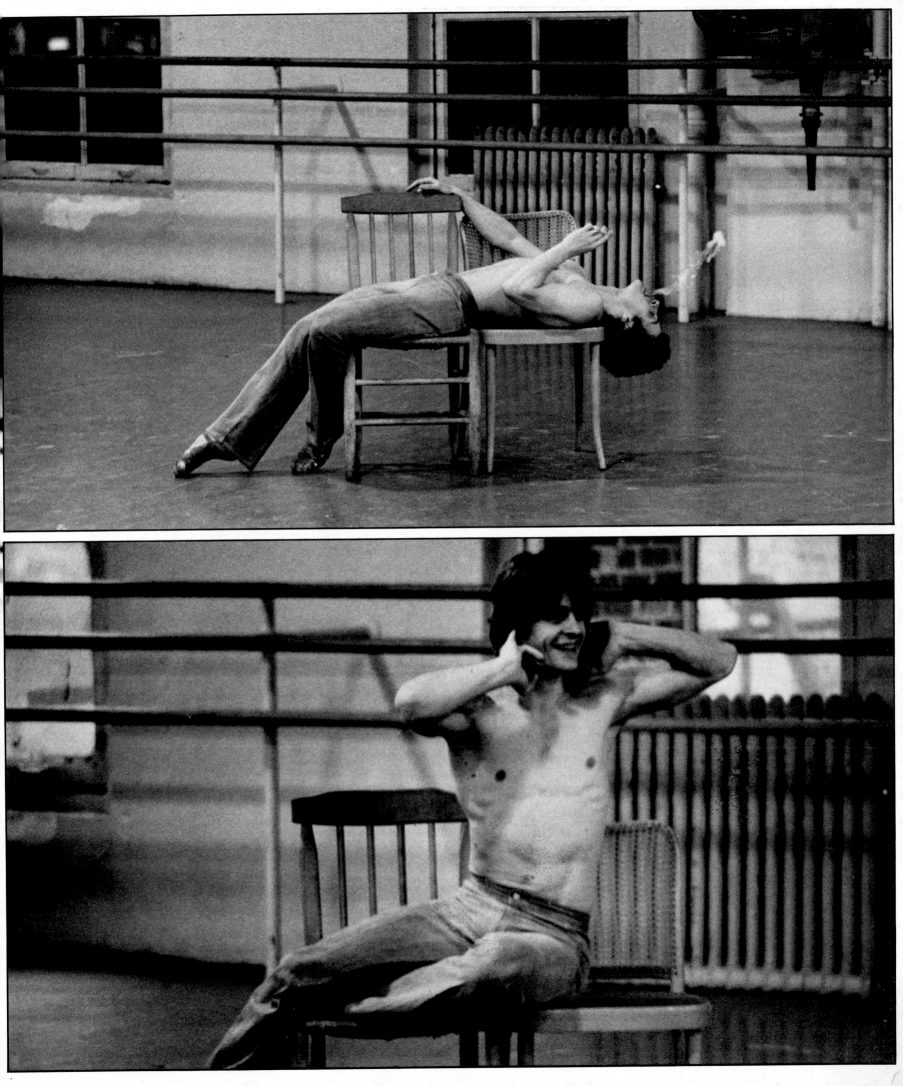

Dancing

They didn't believe in "my" Albrecht for very specific reasons. The traditions, both physical and dramatic, in the way Albrecht is played are very strong in the Soviet Union. Two great interpretations of Albrecht—that of Konstantin Sergeyev at the Kirov and that of Alexei Yermolayev at the Bolshoi—established a standard from as far back as the 1930's. If Sergeyev's Albrecht was the more elegant and poetic and Yermolayev's the more ferocious, they both shared one quality that is basic to all Soviet interpretations: Albrecht is an *aristocrat*. His primary concern is his social position, and his love for Giselle is at best a somewhat serious bagatelle. Albrecht is by implication or intention a cad, and therefore a limited character. His social position and noble bearing are the most important aspects in the standard interpretation of the role.

There were two well-known exceptions to this standardization: the performance by Nikita Dalgushin, a very talented and gifted dancer from the Kirov (who incidentally made a double debut with Natalia Makarova), and by Rudolf Nureyev, who made his debut with Irina Kolpakova. Both interpretations departed significantly from the usual. Unfortunately, by the time I came along these two dancers were no longer with my company. My own models—Yuri Soloviev, Sergei Vikulov, Vladilen Semyonov, all gifted dancers—were still very much in the Sergeyev mold.

I wanted to do *Giselle* very much. I suppose most people consider it mainly a vehicle for a romantic ballerina, but of all the available classics it offers unequaled dramatic opportunities for the male lead. *Giselle* can, in fact, be a two-person drama, and it is the acting that makes the part of Albrecht such a great challenge.

The obstacles I faced in preparing *Giselle,* given the very strict tradition observed in the role, are obvious. I was very young, and looked even younger. My body did not fit the streamlined image of Albrecht. And nobody was convinced that I could do it. So I had something to prove to the directors and myself: I needed to find a way of dancing and miming that was believable and convincing—a way that was more spontaneous and less conceptually restricted.

I discovered for myself the key to a possible change in the entire dramatic architecture of the part. I would start with the premise that Albrecht *really* loves Giselle. This may not sound like such a radical departure, but it was, and I knew it was the only way I might succeed in the role and, by using my own native resources and instinct, resolve the inherent inconsistency imposed by tradition. My goal was to convince both the public and my director that I had a natural right to the part, that I had the ability to create a character I myself could believe in and who would be accepted.

Giselle is not perhaps the most extraordinary ballet ever devised, but it has wonderful opportunities for the dancer to develop. The outlines of the story are so clear, not just in detail but in atmosphere and intent. The steps are simple and effective. The basic material is so uncomplicated that within the given boundaries there are marvelous chances for improvisation. Because the public and the dancers are so familiar with this classic, there is an element of security at the outset that allows for great flexibility in interpretation.

As I said, I began to experiment with *Giselle*. In the past, the rigidly noble interpretation of Albrecht made the ballet into a social drama. *That* Albrecht, no matter where the emphasis was placed (he was either very elegant or very sinister), was basically a negative figure. He exploited Giselle, and then in the second act sought to lift his enormous cloud of guilt. But this interpretation always seemed to me inconsistent with his motives. Inconsistency can be interesting, but in this case it is disorienting. I began from another point entirely. For me Albrecht is so in love with Giselle that his love is his undoing. This love is so true, so perfect, that he does not want to jeopardize it by revealing his true identity. If Giselle knew who he really was, his passion could all too easily be taken to be a kind of *droit du seigneur*. It is the honesty of his feelings that leads him to his dishonesty. But fate steps in, and Albrecht is caught. I want the audience to know that Albrecht is innocent; not that he is not responsible for what occurs, but that his motives are pure.

Act I of *Giselle* is difficult because so much must be accomplished, and so much can happen. I want certain points in the characterization to be very clear. Albrecht knows he isn't what Giselle thinks he is, yet at the same time he is rather insensitive to the whole milieu in which he is moving. When Hilarion is played

as a decent young swain also truly in love with Giselle, the conflict between the two men must be very clearly defined. Hilarion is jealous, and powerfully so. Albrecht is astonished that Hilarion would give him or Giselle trouble. After all, as the prince of the land he is used to getting his own way. It is Hilarion's aggressiveness that throws Albrecht off balance and leads to his first self-betrayal. Little by little he comes to realize that he and his love for Giselle are doomed. When he sees Bathilde's gift to Giselle he doesn't actually recognize it for what it is, but it gives him a jolt, it is a painful reminder to him that he has not told Giselle the truth. At this point the whole conflict is crystalized. Even though Albrecht's love for Giselle is the most important thing in his life, more important than the court and his princely duties, he cannot escape that whole other world. In the climactic final scene, when Hilarion triumphantly reveals Albrecht's secret, Albrecht's over-

whelming instinct is to reassure Giselle of his love. This is much more important
to him than taking revenge on Hilarion. In most versions of the ballet he tries to
kill Hilarion. As I interpret the role, Albrecht suddenly realizes here that Hilarion,
too, loves Giselle. He drops the sword. He wants to tell Giselle the truth and then
is sickened when he sees that there is no point in doing so, that it is too late.

When Bathilde enters Albrecht becomes stony with disappointment and
regret. As he bends to kiss her hand, Giselle forces her way to him and Albrecht
turns from her. He hasn't the strength to face her pain.

The traditional ending for Act I in Russia is for Albrecht to rush offstage. I
have always chosen to remain, to try and seek comfort from those around me.
There is no absolution, but this moment, performed in this way, creates an important bridge to the second act.

*T*he dramatic material of *Giselle,* Act II, is not rich in substance, but with careful preparation and thought it can be meaningful. One basic consideration is that of maintaining a balance with the spirit, the Wili Giselle. The Act II Giselle demands a careful stylization and delicacy that precludes heavy dramatics, and it is very easy — and very destructive — for the Albrecht to grab all the attention. The way I see it, Albrecht's task is now to adapt to the world of the Wilis. Once he realizes he is faced with another dimension, he desperately wants to communicate with it, to hold on to it in some way. So he must enter that world, believe in it, absorb it. He must also meet its standards. The Wilis express their power in dance. Their Queen's dance is bold and full of awesome strength. So Albrecht's dance must be strong too, as strong as possible. Once he sees Giselle as a spirit, he doesn't run away from her; he accepts her new state. He projects himself into her world. I want to make this transition clear. I know that many of these ideas do not translate literally to an audience, do not always come across, but they help me believe in the role as I feel it should be. The transition Albrecht makes from the real world to that of the Wilis begins the moment he dances *with* the Wili Giselle.

After that the task is relatively simple. The story makes the necessary demands. Albrecht fights to hold on to Giselle and fights to live.

It is difficult to maintain the sense of balance throughout, however. There must be no sharp turns, no radical departures once the mood is established. Albrecht must try to blend with Giselle. The flowers are crucial. They mean so many things to him: they are a symbol of his pain and they are a symbol of Giselle, too. Giselle expresses herself through flowers when she dances with the lilies, throwing them to him as if to say, "Yes, these flowers are a part of me. They are me. I know you must have them." And then later Giselle again uses the flowers to appease Myrtha, the Queen of the Wilis. Here it's as if she says, "See how strong my bond with this man is. Take these flowers and know it."

Finally, the flowers are central to the end of the whole drama. When Albrecht is saved and Giselle has forgiven him but must return to the world of the Wilis, Albrecht desperately tries to hold on to her. The way of that world cannot be halted, but in strewing the flowers in a straight line from her grave Albrecht tries to save her for himself, to hold on to the final link between them.

La Bayadère

Choreography by Marius Petipa. Music by Leon Minkus. First performance: Maryinsky Theatre, Saint Petersburg, January 23, 1877. Current American Ballet Theatre production, Kingdom of the Shades scene (1974), staged by Natalia Makarova. Costumes by Marcos Paredes. First performed by Baryshnikov, New York, August 5, 1974, with Natalia Makarova; also danced with Gelsey Kirkland and Noella Pontois.

I rehearsed the role of Solor in *La Bayadère* in Russia with Natalia Dudinskaya, the famous Kirov ballerina, but I never danced it there. I also rehearsed the part with Natalia Makarova, but we were unable to perform it.

Chabukiani, the famous Russian virtuoso, had rechoreographed the second act in the 1940's, and created a very elaborate male solo to be included in the *pas d'action,* or wedding celebration scene. This was a famous variation using a bow and arrow, as if the dancer was showing off his skill as a hunter at the wedding; it was a great triumph for male dancing in the Soviet Union. After Chabukiani retired from dancing, the bow and arrow were no longer kept by the male dancers in the Kirov, and the variation was danced without them, which was not terribly good, because the sense was lost.

When the third act is given alone, as American Ballet Theatre and the Royal Ballet do it, there is a need for an additional male variation, so this one from Act II is used. I was taught this variation by my teacher Pushkin for the Moscow Competitions in 1969. Basically the choreography as we know it from Makarova's staging for American Ballet Theatre is completely authentic.

La Bayadère is one of the great, if not the greatest, classical works in the history of ballet. It is Petipa's idea of life in the beyond, a world of peace, dignity, symmetry, and harmony — a world that can be fully explained and presented through the medium of the finest classical choreographic and dance techniques. Dramatically, this third act is very beautiful. It opens with an hypnotic entrance for the corps de ballet that immediately suggests the peace and unity of the Shades' kingdom. Their entrance is followed by that of the three principal Shades, whose variations are very brilliantly and uniquely characterized — one is a light allegro, one a heavier allegro, and one a very beautiful adagio.

Solor is then introduced. You must remember that this whole scene is slightly out of context; in the full-length version you understand that this is Solor's opium dream — his fantasy trip into the beyond to retrieve Nikia, the woman he loved more than anything on earth. Solor is a passionate and romantic figure, a great lover. And Nikia is introduced as the link between the warm, romantic real world and the never-never land of the Kingdom of the Shades. She is a link with the dead and the symbol of female purity and perfection. She is Innocence. Solor tries to bring her back into the real world and keep her, but she is always beyond him, just above him. (You will notice in the choreography that Nikia is most of the time either in front of Solor or just above him in lifts, always in some way slightly out of reach.) She embodies all the classic female virtues: loyalty, self-sacrifice, serenity. What is so wonderful about *La Bayadère* is the extraordinary dry purity of the classical steps combined with the grandest of romantic notions.

In dancing Solor I of course work knowing the implications of the role in the complete ballet. Solor is a tormented, searching man, wild with the need to find perfect love. I'm sure when I come rushing on as Solor that the audience thinks, "Well, who needs *him*?" after that extraordinary opening for the corps de ballet.

La Bayadère is unique; it is a self-contained world with its own rules, where everything is explained in a pure and harmonious style. All of Petipa's great choreographic hallmarks are there — the semi-circles, the wedges, the horizontals — all his finely wrought architectural sense is seen in full bloom. Poetically it is unmatched in the classical repertory.

Don Quixote
Pas de deux

Choreography by Marius Petipa. Music by Leon Minkus. First performance: Bolshoi Theatre, Moscow, December 26, 1869. For American Ballet Theatre, Baryshnikov dances the grand pas de deux in the Kirov version. First performance, New York, August 9, 1974, with Natalia Makarova; also danced with Gelsey Kirkland and Noella Pontois.

Don Quixote was the first full-length ballet I performed in the Soviet Union. Giving the pas de deux out of context makes it a very different kind of theatrical exercise. It is an *exam* — with the public as the examiner — in virtuosity, taste, and personality. There is a certain amount of controversy, in Russia if not here, about deviation from the original choreography (which still exists); but as a classical showpiece it has been altered considerably over the years. When I first performed the pas de deux I danced it in its most refined version, with only a few minor changes. This original version is more *classical*; there is little exaggeration and the steps are very simple. *Don Quixote* is a ballet that combines strict classical technique and a style with *caractère* feeling, and when the pas de deux is performed in context with the entire work it becomes the ultimate expression of the *classical* element, and seems particularly ``pure.'' But when it is performed alone, as a showpiece, one must make it a dramatic ``profile,'' since the characterization has not been established.

In the Soviet Union the role of Don Basilio was always danced most successfully by dancers of great personality, such as Messerer and Yermalayev of the
Bolshoi, who kept within a very strict classical style. In our time it is the Bolshoi's
Vladimir Vasiliev who has been responsible for changing the nature of this role so
drastically. He inserted steps into the great pas de deux – double *sauts de basque*,
for example, and the combination of jeté, then a *grand battement* through first

position, *sauté*, and fouetté into attitude — that would have been inconceivable in the early postwar years, and over a period of time he has left his mark on the part. Vasiliev's influence, however, was not felt so much at the Kirov.

I had learned the *Don Quixote* pas de deux while I was still in the Kirov school, and later I was coached for the full-length production by Kurgapkina, who had danced the leading role of Kitri with great success, and who was one of the

company's major ballerinas. At first I was terribly green. It was a great change for me to appear in a part that had such long pantomime sequences, such comic touches—and four *long* acts. But *Don Quixote* was very important to me as experience in learning the ways of the stage.

Doing the pas de deux by itself is always an experiment. There is a great deal of leeway possible in the actual steps, but the framework of the character is quite clear. It is a challenge to communicate a feeling of classical style together with a sense of humor and charm without distorting either. If the *Don Quixote* pas de deux is performed exclusively as a brute technical tour de force the sense of the dance may very well be lost. You must always keep a pas de deux like this within sensible boundaries, yet make it fun; combine pure dance with virtuosity, with style, with humor. But keep it from becoming a circus. There is tremendous pressure on the performers in this pas de deux. You have a short, very short amount of time in which you must dance with tremendous power and energy and style. You have only a few minutes to create a complete theatrical event.

Dancing the virtuoso classical pas de deux may not be a crucial artistic experience, but they do serve a purpose. They keep the dancer in shape, keyed up, in tone. And besides, audiences love them!

Coppélia

Choreography by Arthur Saint-Leon. Music by Leo Delibes. First performance: Paris, May 25, 1870. Current American Ballet Theatre production (1968) choreographed by Enrique Martinez, after Saint-Leon. Scenery and costumes by William Pitkin. First performed by Baryshnikov, Washington, D.C., October 27, 1974, with Gelsey Kirkland; also danced with Natalia Makarova.

I had never danced the role of Franz in *Coppélia* in the Soviet Union because the full-length ballet is no longer in the repertory. I did perform the grand pas de deux, which has remained a standard classical divertissement. There is really no tradition for this kind of "classical" comedy role in Russia; in fact, I never prepared or danced *any* full comic part there. The only full-length *Coppélia* I had ever seen was Alicia Alonso's production for the National Ballet of Cuba. When I arrived in America I was taught the role by Enrique Martinez, who had choreographed *Coppélia* for American Ballet Theatre.

Coppélia is perhaps not one of the really great classics, and yet it is enormously popular — for its lightness, its humor, and, above all, for its charming score. More than any other classic, it may be a vehicle for its leading dancers; its basic material can be molded in many surprising ways. Working in a ballet like this is always very interesting. You have the outlines, the basic ingredients of a story in which a great deal of dramatic improvisation can be developed. You have the challenge of being funny but not farcical, of working with a partner in pantomime and of developing the characterization spontaneously each time you perform.

The role of Franz is not terribly complicated. He is a flirt; he flirts with *everyone*. Failing to recognize Swanilda's will of iron, he assumes that she is just a silly little girl. Her caprices tickle his fancy, he is amused by her, fascinated by her, but he doesn't take her seriously — which leads to all his problems. His antics are designed to provoke her, because he understands just how teasable she is. Traditionally Franz is played as a real dolt. I choose to play him as if that doltish quality masks a loving appreciation of his sparring partner, his true love Swanilda. He knows what a silly goose she can be, and he has the power to make her jealous — and he enjoys doing so.

Potentially the ideas behind *Coppélia* are fascinating. There are many different ways in which these ideas can be developed. And the character of Doctor Coppelius is one of the most compelling in the ballet repertory. *Coppélia* is really *his* tragedy. You have these young, unprincipled, spoiled people who ridicule and destroy a man's greatest dream. And through that experience . . . they mature. They become responsible adults. In showing this you can ennoble a charming romantic comedy.

Perhaps I will enjoy dancing in this ballet more when I am mature enough to be playing Doctor Coppelius, not Franz!

Theme and Variations

Choreography by George Balanchine. Music by Peter Tchaikovsky. First performance by American Ballet Theatre, New York, November 26, 1947, with Alicia Alonso and Igor Youskevitch. Current American Ballet Theatre production 1958. Scenery by Eugene Dunkel after Bibiena. Costumes by André Levasseur. First performed by Baryshnikov, Washington, D.C., October 30, 1974, with Gelsey Kirkland.

I prepared *Theme and Variations* with the help of Michael Land, ballet master of American Ballet Theatre, and of Gelsey Kirkland. I had seen *Theme* danced in Leningrad when the New York City Ballet appeared there in 1972, with Gelsey dancing the ballerina role. When I was working on the ballet several years later Gelsey was extremely helpful, but *Theme and Variations* was and remains the most difficult ballet I have performed since I came to the West.

I had basically been used to roles with very large, open movements. *Theme* demanded a new strict control as well as enormous power and precision in the legs. The first time I danced it I thought my legs would drop off. There is a continuous stream of demi-plié and plié, down, up, down, up, tension, release, tension, release. And that, coupled with working from a very accentuated turn-out at all times, means that the strain on the legs is incredible.

The choreography for the male variations requires a certain unrelenting level of energy; there is very little rest, a constant build to the climax. One diagonal of very difficult beats leads immediately into a continuously repeated beat-*sissonne* combination and then into seven double tours alternating with pirouettes, ending with a multiple pirouette. All this great physical challenge gives enormous physical pleasure, even more so because the choreography is so profoundly musical and therefore "natural." The strict musical timing that took me so long to master is inevitable, and therefore seems almost more ideally perfect than one could ever dream of.

The pas de deux is particularly extraordinary, with its two contained but brilliant personalities. It is like a fantastic walk, a fantastic promenade — so alive, so lively. And yet the atmosphere of *Theme and Variations* is one of modest, peaceful grandeur. When you dance it, you assume an enormous responsibility. You feel that you are an instrument. It is like being a terribly vital screw or nail, knowing that if you fail everything will fall apart. There is no time to think, you have to go out and do it, and do it right. In one sense, dancing *Theme* does not require great initiative. You have to forget yourself, lose yourself in the choreography, which is, as I've said, the inevitable resolution of that particular music.

When I first danced this part I learned a tremendous amount from watching Gelsey, because she knew so well how to pace the ballet. She had learned how to create this marvelous atmosphere of reserve, of harmony, and at the same time to project the clarity and brilliance, the fireworks. Dancing *Theme and Variations* was the realization for me of a dream. I had seen several Balanchine works and I knew and know that I wanted to dance as many of them as possible. Beginning with *Theme and Variations* was perhaps beginning at a very advanced level; it is, after all, the summation of Balanchine's neo-classical style. Yet I was lucky to begin where I did, even if it was as difficult for me as it was. I have much more Balanchine to dance before it is all over.

Les Patineurs

Choreography by Frederick Ashton. Music by Giacomo Meyerbeer. First performance by the Vic-Wells (now the Royal) Ballet, London, February 16, 1937, with Harold Turner. Current American Ballet Theatre production 1946. Scenery and costumes by Cecil Beaton. First performed by Baryshnikov, New York, December 26, 1974.

I first saw *Les Patineurs* on television in the Soviet Union, and still remembered it extremely clearly when I began to prepare the role of the Green Skater. My principal coach was the late Fiorella Keane, who knew it from her days with the Royal Ballet.

The most exciting thing about *Les Patineurs* is that Ashton has taken a skating party in all seriousness. He understands how important a social ritual such a party can be. Even though the ballet is technically a classical — or neo-classical — divertissement, it really captures both the atmosphere of a skating pond and the feeling of a period. There's a special gaiety, a special brisk happiness in the air. The choreography for the Green Skater is extremely versatile and physically very difficult. It puts a tremendous strain on one's breathing. It moves around a lot. For example, the Green Skater's big variation is immediately followed by his pas de trois with the two girls. In this pas de trois I have a great many very small, low sautées and ronds de jambe, and it is hard to maintain the delicacy, precision, and power of these steps when you're winded. It's hard, but it's also a challenge. Not only does the Green Skater have to give the impression of enormous speed, he also has to create the illusion of wearing skates, which demands constant attention to precision. Pirouettes as pirouettes are not enough, they must be especially clean in order

to confirm this impression of being on skates. And there is also the matter of accelerating and de-accelerating tempo, to give the illusion of spinning as a skater spins.

There is a very difficult moment in this ballet — the famous butterfly jump — which in fact presented severe problems for me. I found it to be the typical movement of a gymnast, rather like doing a cartwheel without hands. It's an interesting and effective step, but I just couldn't manage it. I suppose if I had had a much longer time to prepare the role I would have found a way, but instead I replaced it with a split jump in the air.

Les Patineurs is a great vignette. Poetically — and balletically — it works so well because Ashton has been able to find a *demi-caractère* style that is based on classical steps. The character of the Green Skater is festive, exciting, exuberant; he is a man without discipline who dashes in unexpectedly, an independent soul in a very civilized world. The first time I danced the part I attempted it more in a character vein, using a very heavy make-up with freckles. I made more faces; I used a red nose. After the first performance I abandoned all that, because the characterization is in the role, it's in the steps. You just don't need all that extra artificiality. The conceit is so well observed and the atmosphere so fine that it can only be a great "lift" to appear in *Les Patineurs*.

La Fille Mal Gardée

Choreography by Jean Dauberval. Music by Peter Ludwig Hertel. First performance: Bordeaux, 1789. Current American Ballet Theatre production (1972) choreographed by Dimitri Romanoff, after Dauberval. Scenery and costumes by Rolf Gerard. First performed by Baryshnikov, New York, December 28, 1974, with Natalia Makarova; also danced with Gelsey Kirkland.

La Fille Mal Gardée, as opposed to *Coppélia,* is a ballet that does have a tradition in the Soviet Union. Even though I had never danced the role of Colin before, I knew that "world," that tradition of classical vaudeville — very, very light, very funny. I decided to work in a *very* broad style I had never attempted before. The sillier the situation became, the more raucous the pantomime, the more potentially interesting it was for me as an exercise in humor and logic. But *Fille* and its leading male role do not particularly appeal to me; there are elements of the grotesque in the characterization and plot that I don't find natural to my temperament and abilities. There's a heavy dose of irony, rather nasty irony, in this ballet, which makes it difficult for me to grab hold of the character.

The situation in a piece like this has to be made funny, but funny *for the audience,* without the dancer seeming to be commenting on the humor. This is more difficult than it may appear. You can get carried away with the farcical aspect of the role and fail to be sensitive to the impact it is having. It's funny only if it's performed without vulgarity, and it's not easy to hit the right balance all the time.

The major difficulty — and contradiction — here is that the ballet's natural impulse is toward farce, while the character of Colin is essentially conceived as that of a romantic hero, genuinely in love with Lise and upset that she is being forced to marry a halfwit. The dancer must both retain the romantic style and help to create the farcical atmosphere. I find this tension disagreeable.

La Sylphide

Choreography by August Bournonville. Music by Hermann von Løvenskjold. First performance by the Royal Danish Ballet, Copenhagen, 1836. Current American Ballet Theatre production (1965) choreographed by Erik Bruhn after Bournonville. Scenery and costumes by Robert O'Hearn. First performed by Baryshnikov, New York, January 4, 1975, with Gelsey Kirkland; also danced with Natalia Makarova.

I had seen American Ballet Theatre's production of *La Sylphide* with Toni Lander and Royes Fernandez as well as the Royal Danish Ballet's version with Peter Schaufuss, and when I came to the West I immediately asked to dance it.

Everything about dancing Bournonville's ballets is different from what I have been trained to do. In Bournonville one is searching for a very reserved, refined stylistic voice, and yet one still wants to keep as much excitement as possible in the dancing. The technique is very unusual; it demands extraordinary flexibility in the legs and a kind of static torso. When I first began dancing this ballet my "classical habits" kept interfering; even something as simple as a run is different in Bournonville than in classical Russian style. When I had mastered the steps of *Sylphide* I still asked for an inordinate number of extra rehearsals because I felt it might not be as theatrically exciting as it ought to be. But as I became more and more familiar with the precision and cleanliness of the technique, as the rules which govern this world became absorbed into my body, I felt much better about it.

Just a few words on the technical aspects of this role: there are many, many jumps in Bournonville, many beats, entrechats, et cetera. The *épaulement* is extremely limited, so that as you move you feel you're dancing with your legs and nothing else. Erik Bruhn worked with me and gave me extremely good and detailed corrections, showing me how to reach the necessary balance of softness and strength in the many jumps and how to perform the role in general. For example, he showed me how to achieve what I would call a "soft startle" at the waking up of James in the first act.

There's enormous physical pleasure in dancing Bournonville. The style and the steps are so harmonious, so complete, that you instantly recognize in your mind and in your body a great classical tradition. The simplicity of it and the emotional tranquility are extremely satisfying.

On to the story. *La Sylphide* is a "realistic" fairy tale. James lives in a world that accepts sylphs and witches as a natural phenomenon. Good and evil are extremely conventional, much more conventional than, say, in *Giselle*. At the beginning of *La Sylphide,* as James sleeps, the Sylph is trying to get into his mind. When he moves restlessly in his chair as she dances so brilliantly around the room, she's "getting through" to him. He, of course, is not sure that it has really happened. He is still preoccupied with his first encounter with the Sylph when his mortal fiancée, Effie, kisses him. He remembers as if in a dream; he senses that something is happening and then when he sees the Sylph through the window his reaction is, "Oh well, she's *real.*" The Sylph is very unhappy that he is marrying Effie, but James is a responsible adult who has an obligation to Effie, even though he is completely fascinated with the Sylph.

*I*n the long scene between James and the Sylph we see that he in fact begins to tire of her coquetry and jealousy, and feels that he must be honest toward Effie. And once again he's perplexed. The Sylph abandons her sad mood and says, "Let's dance." He is so surprised at this quick change in her mood that he is completely disarmed. The more she teases and tries to slip away from him, the more he wants her.

Perhaps the most interesting character in the entire ballet is the Witch. The whole story of *La Sylphide* unfolds as if it had been told by her. She is in complete control of herself and of the situation from the moment she enters. She has selected her victims, and she knows everything. James reacts more powerfully to her than to anything in his life — he knows instinctively that she is evil. When the Witch asks to warm her hands, James panics. He knows that she's dangerous and that he's got to get rid of her. He is terrified that she will do irrevocable damage. This whole scene is brilliantly conceived as a long pantomime between James and the Witch, both of whom know what's taking place. He goes through the charade of accepting her and letting her tell the fortunes, all the while terrified of her power. He knows that she is indeed a Witch. But when the Sylph returns at the end of the act he loses all sense of reason. His fear of the Witch and his love of Effie both pale as the delicious enchantment of this fairy creature mesmerizes him. (It is, after all, a romantic tale.) He leaves to go with her to the woods.

The second act begins on a delightful note — the Sylph takes James into her "house." And he thinks, "Oh, I've hit upon a nice upper-class sylphide." Hers is a very nice glade. She brings on her "sewing circle," teasing him, always slipping away from him, always putting something between him and herself. His frustration mounts. Then, of course, there's the long, brilliant dancing section and finally

James's second scene with the Witch. He still recognizes her for what she is, but no longer fears anything. He has become the great romantic egoist, spoiled and selfish like a child. He must have a present to attract the Sylph, and he's too blind to see what's being done to him. The Witch is in control. Of course, the whole thing ends in tragedy; the Sylph dies from the poisoned scarf and James is left with nothing but an ugly sense of reality as he watches Effie pass by. He has failed because of his romantic notions. The power of his ideals, his need for perfection, have done him in completely. James is always searching for the great romance, for poetry and beauty in this life, and the Sylph embodied all that for him.

There's something else as well: the normal point of view is really set up against James. From the way things work out we draw the conclusion that one should not go after the impossible and the superficial.

The world of *La Sylphide* is a wonderful whole, with its great dancing from a great tradition and with its marvelous score. The music is very good dance music in the first place, and beyond that it contains *a secret*. It is naïve, but it has sudden and startling depths. It is also dramatically very accurate.

The dancing sections of *La Sylphide* are in many ways both parallel to and independent of the story. You must be very careful when dancing not to use too much dramatic emphasis in the "set" pieces, which are indeed very stylized. This doesn't mean that there isn't a general atmosphere to be maintained in which something of the drama can be expressed, but a very delicate balance between drama and dance must be sustained. If I had to decide between *La Sylphide* and *Giselle* as to which was the greater romantic ballet or as to which was the most satisfying to perform — I just couldn't choose.

Le Jeune Homme et la Mort

Choreography by Roland Petit. Music by Johann Sebastian Bach. Scenery and costumes by Georges Wakhevitch. First performance by Ballets des Champs-Elysées, Paris, June 25, 1946, with Jean Babilée and Nathalie Philippart. Current American Ballet Theatre production (1951) first performed by Baryshnikov, New York, January 9, 1975, with Bonnie Mathis.

It was actually Antony Tudor who suggested that I do *Le Jeune Homme et la Mort* — "a new experience that might intrigue you." The idea rang very true, and I asked if it could be done. I was interested not only because it was different, but because it would be the first really non-classical role I had ever prepared and danced in my life. Having just come to the West, it was fascinating for me to begin working on a piece like this.

I knew about Roland Petit in Russia, and we were familiar with his famous works — *Notre Dame de Paris, La Croqueuse de Diamants, Carmen,* and many others. And we knew something about the artistic atmosphere and the people surrounding Roland after the war; about Jean Babilée, Zizi Jeanmaire, and all the others. Roland prepared the ballet with me very carefully. He is a marvelous, cultured, expansive man. He was able to re-create the period for me just by talking. He told me of that whole postwar neurosis, the exposed nerves, the "agony of art," the idea of living in "the world as a private fantasy."

Roland's careful preparation was not only verbal; he himself rehearsed Bonnie Mathis and me from beginning to end. He insisted on changing a great deal of the choreography because he felt I was so different from Babilée temperamentally, physically, and technically, that to re-create the steps as they had been created for Babilée made no sense. I was very concerned about these changes, but Roland insisted that the ballet had to be true to *my* abilities. From what I have read and what I know of Babilée, I suspect he was much more neurotic, much more explosive onstage than I was. But I think Roland also found a way of making the role interesting as seen through me.

I consider *Jeune Homme* a successful "popular" ballet. True, it is a period piece, but the questions it raises are timeless; if it is perhaps a cliché, it has the *force* of a cliché. It is about loneliness, and it is a naturalistic as well as a surrealistic drama: pure Cocteau. Roland used Cocteau's libretto, retaining the most important aspects of the story and strengthening them. I think their collaboration worked perfectly. Roland understood how to use the peculiar theatricality of Cocteau's story and, at the same time, make it clearer for the stage.

The symbolic conflict in *Jeune Homme* is the conflict between love and death; how there is great beauty in love and great beauty in death. For the young man, death represents a release from enormous pain, rejection, dark loneliness; love is something that imprisons the spirit even as it frees it. It is death that achieves the ultimate liberation.

Though it is a very satisfying ballet to perform, *Jeune Homme* is both difficult and tiring. The ballet demands great virtuosity; it contains many difficult combinations and leaps and spins and turns, and it is very hard on the breathing, as you must run all over the stage, all over the furniture, all over the room, all over the ceiling practically by the time it's over. Also, the steps are not set on the beat but are arranged in groups that then must fit within a given time sequence. This is a challenge, because a certain amount of improvisation becomes an integral part of the piece.

Jeune Homme was very important to me when I first performed it. The idea of embodying so much pain and loneliness; the tense contrast between relief at and horror of the beautiful woman who both represents joy and brings one to the point of suicide — this all appealed to me. And I do love that final moment when the walls go up and death turns from being a terrifying thing into a profoundly moving and positive force leading the artist into a pure world....

Le Corsaire
Pas de deux

Choreography by Marius Petipa. Music by Riccardo Drigo. First performance: Maryinsky Theatre, Saint Petersburg, January 25, 1899. For American Ballet Theatre, Baryshnikov dances the grand pas de deux in the Kirov version. First performance, New York, January 11, 1975, with Gelsey Kirkland.

I was still at the Kirov School when I first learned the variation and pas de deux from *Le Corsaire.* My teacher Pushkin coached me in the role, and while I was still in the Soviet Union I danced it with several ballerinas: Alla Sizova, Olga Vtorushina, and Svetlana Yefremova. The choreography is totally Petipa's, and purer than, for example, the *Don Quixote* pas de deux, which has undergone certain changes over the years. The choreography for *Le Corsaire,* on the other hand, has been passed down more cleanly from one generation to the next, and we believe that it is very accurate. The variations for the male dancer especially, with comparatively few alterations, are almost as they were in the days of Petipa, and I dance the adagio now exactly as Pushkin showed it to me.

*M*usically there have been many versions presented in the West. For a number of years, that staged by Rudolf Nureyev was accepted as the standard, but the version Nureyev had performed earlier with Sizova used music for the ballerina's variation taken from the Queen of the Dryad's dance in *Don Quixote*. When I danced the pas de deux with Gelsey Kirkland the music for her variation was the original.

As in the *Don Quixote* pas de deux, the characterization and style of *Le Corsaire* save the dance from being just a dry, classical exercise. One is able to bring to it the knowledge and conviction of the full-length *Corsaire*, with all its grand romantic ideas.

The story of *Le Corsaire* is that of a Greek girl, Medora, who has been abducted by Conrad, a pirate chief. Conrad, which is basically a mime role, orders his favorite slave to dance with Medora to keep her happy. This pas de deux is distinguished by many symbolic gestures and poses of subjugation. Apart from this, it's simply a beautiful, classical romance.

Technically the demands of *Le Corsaire* are very straightforward, virtuoso classical steps and combinations. It is a difficult pas de deux to perform, but perhaps not as challenging as certain others. This slave is not my favorite classical virtuoso role.

Choreography by Leonid Jacobson. Music by Genaidi Banschikov. First performance: International Ballet Competitions, Moscow, June, 1969, with Baryshnikov. First performance by American Ballet Theatre, Washington, D.C., May 20, 1975 (costume by Carl Michell), with Baryshnikov.

When I knew that I needed a specially choreographed piece for the international Moscow competition in 1969 I insisted on Leonid Jacobson. He had been a dancer at the Kirov and subsequently became the most interesting choreographer working with the company on a consistent basis. His great talent lay in the complexity and variety of movement styles he was able to develop; he had a special knack for creating steps and characterizations ideally suited to the dancers. In other words, his work did not imprison the performer, but always seemed able to reveal new, *true* aspects of his potential.

Jacobson chose the subject of Vestris for particular reasons. First of all, he believed that Vestris was an appropriate choice historically — a very versatile and fascinating character in the history of ballet. And then he recognized that a dance based on Vestris was a valid *theatrical* idea: Vestris was noted for his versatility in acting as well as for his dancing technique, and that gave Jacobson a chance to create a series of dramatic vignettes in a style appropriate to the depiction of a myth.

Jacobson and I studied all the lithographs of Vestris very carefully, and examined the books available in our good libraries. There were many French texts of the period that had engravings of Vestris, and we were fortunately able to utilize the special poses and dramatic attitudes they illustrated. We also studied contemporary porcelain figures and sculpture in the Hermitage Museum. But the idea was not to re-create Vestris *literally*, which would have been impossible: Vestris is much like Nijinsky — a great deal has been written about him but very little is known about what he actually did. Instead, Jacobson wanted to create the feeling of a phenomenon, someone *like* Vestris, who was famous for his mime technique, his ability to switch very easily from one character to another and his talent for amusing the aristocracy with his sometimes unpleasant caricaturizations of the members of the court. At the same time, he was a great virtuoso dancer. Jacobson put all these things together in such a way that this solo is both *of* Vestris and *about* Vestris.

Although Vestris was a great improviser, Jacobson did not allow for improvisation in this piece (even though as you perform it more and more, the spontaneity of each performance affects the nature of the vignettes). He set everything extremely precisely and in great detail, down to facial expressions and hand gestures, and he worked very closely with his young, talented composer.

Each vignette was mapped out to take approximately fifteen seconds. There were twelve of them at first, twelve music sections and twelve dance sections, but later this was cut. Each of these vignettes is a dialogue between the performer and his audience. The exceptions are at the beginning and the end, which are two "framing" pieces performed in a very classical style — not classical in the sense of the late-nineteenth-century classical ballet technique, but classical in relationship to the rest of the pieces, which are much more humanized and natural. The idea was to re-create several different personages who, we hoped, would demonstrate both the versatility of the dancer — that's me — and of the historical figure.

*I*t was presumptuous of me to do this part. I wasn't convinced that I would be at all successful, but, in forcing me to try to be so tremendously versatile in this way, Jacobson taught me an enormous amount. And to go through each vignette specifically is to see that Jacobson created not only a mime equivalent for each character but a dance equivalent as well.

The first vignette is the old man whose dance is characterized by broken-down little steps and old-man gestures. The second is the young coquette who minces and bats her eyelashes, and whose dance is characterized by frivolous, light little beats. She's on the make. The third is the preacher, who has very bold, large movements, a lot of deep bending and pliéing; and then there is the Vestris dance, which stresses the forceful beats and turns and light jumps Vestris was famous for. Then comes the praying woman who for most of the time is on her knees with her arms stretched toward heaven. Then there is the laughing man who is drunk, and all of whose steps are off balance. And last there is the dying old man who depends on his cane to hold him up and who finally falls to the ground dead.

Jacobson's intent is very, very clear. Each section is beautifully set up, using an almost complete blackout technique, and each characterization is swiftly and finely drawn. The dance also successfully mixes period style and detail with a contemporary accent and modulation that makes the whole thing more than just a precious bauble.

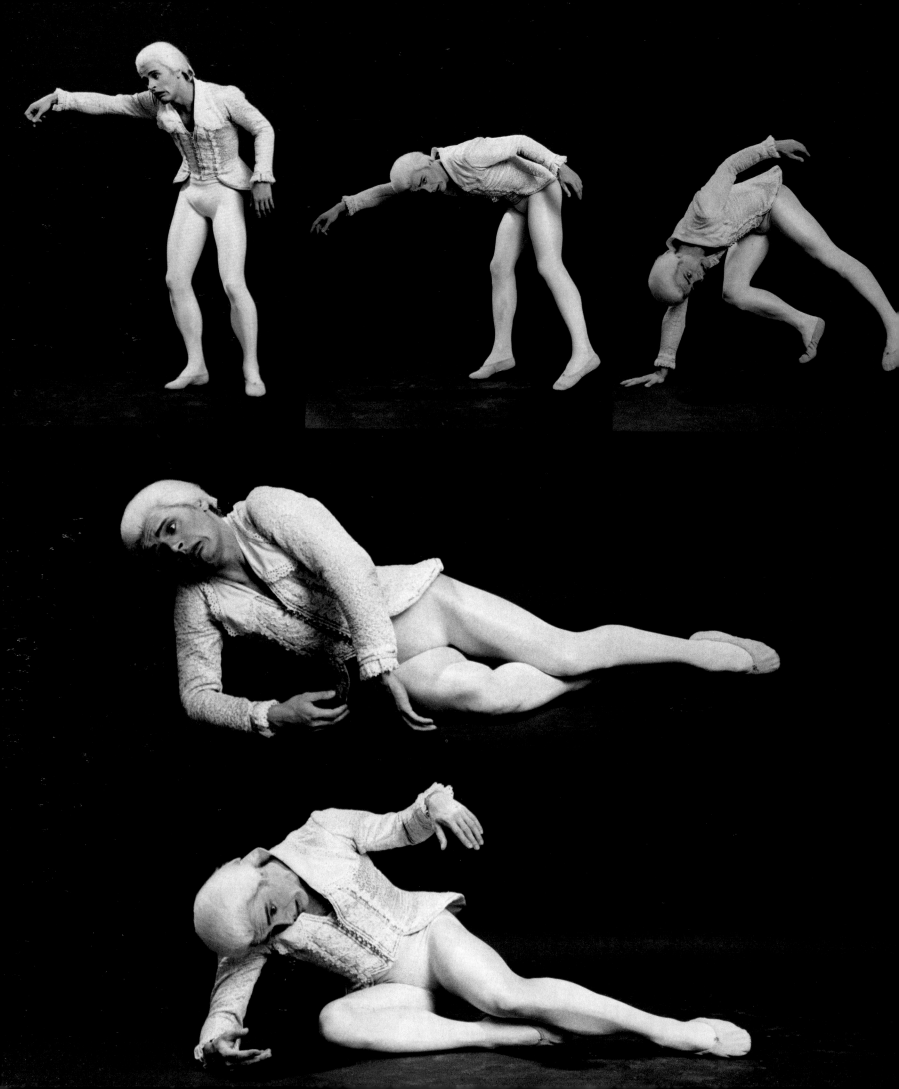

Choreography by John Butler. Music by Samuel Barber. First performance: Spoleto Festival, June 28, 1975, with Baryshnikov and Carla Fracci. First performance by American Ballet Theatre, New York, January 13, 1976, costumes and scenery by Rouben Ter-Arutunian, with Baryshnikov and Fracci; also danced with Marcia Haydée.

Although I had seen John Butler's *After Eden* and *Sebastian* on videotape, I had no idea of what he wished to do with *Medea*. I assumed that if it were going to be a pas de deux, one character would be Jason, and that would be me. When we began working it became immediately obvious that Butler knew exactly what he wanted, and had a clear understanding of the music. The choreography is very organic, and flows naturally from the music — the kind of relationship between music and score that is always the most rewarding. John Butler uses classical positions and steps; he has a brilliant understanding of the classical technique. But in *Medea* he uses it in combination with a Graham-like style, which was of course fascinating to me.

At first it was difficult for me to execute John's ideas, but in the end it became very natural. What *was* difficult was accenting the movement the way he wanted me to. I had to discover the edgy, sharp tone, and to incorporate the stretched, parallel arms and hands and the demi-contractions of the Graham style into the classical technique that was the basic language of the work — always maintaining the extreme precision of movement that John demands.

Although there is no developed story in this pas de deux, it reveals the atmosphere and the "information" of the Medea legend. It describes the relationship of two people in a specific context. A charged, electric feeling is created, rather than the literal interpretation of a story. The ballet gives the impression of re-creating both dialogue and monologue.

Butler has a give-and-take attitude, one of equality with the dancer, and his working style is relaxed and clear. He responded so ardently to Barber's gripping score, with its warm dramatic power that is so exciting to dance to, that I enjoyed every minute of working with him. I even enjoyed rehearsing!

Shadowplay

Choreography by Antony Tudor. Music by Charles Koechlin. Scenery and costumes by Michael Annals. First performance by the Royal Ballet, London, January 25, 1967, with Anthony Dowell, Merle Park, and Derek Rencher. First performance by American Ballet Theatre, New York, July 23, 1975, with Baryshnikov, Gelsey Kirkland, and Jonas Kage.

I had never seen *Shadowplay* but I had read about it; Christopher Newton taught me the steps. The unfolding of the story is very simple and clear. It tells of a boy who is at ease, who is relaxed, who is ready to experience meditation. He is the son of Buddha and has *that* attitude. Tudor himself gave me several books on Zen Buddhism, as well as photographs showing the preparations for meditating.

In *Shadowplay* you must project a kind of above-it-all (in this case above-the-monkeys) attitude. The boy is constantly being disturbed, but only in a sort of irritating, needly way. First the monkeys, then the girls, come out to distract him from his true purpose. And then comes the other man, the King of the Jungle, who is a kind of symbol for all that is distracting in the world. The boy tries desperately to escape from the hypnotic emotional and physical power of this man; they fight,

and the boy wins. Then the big monkeys bring the woman onstage. They dance a pas de deux. She is leading him on, tying him up; taking him away from his spiritual peace, and involving him physically. Suddenly she abandons him, leaving him suspended in mid-air. He becomes completely disoriented. Hyperactive. The girl returns, and they dance an antagonistic pas de deux in which all his resentment against her and the monkeys is expressed. He reacts to the bad aura of it all; he realizes that they're "trouble," and resists them. The King of the Jungle returns, and the boy conquers him completely, assuming a position of mental and physical dominance. *He* is now the strongest in the jungle. There is a brief triumphant march to the throne. The monkeys part before the boy as he assumes his regal meditating position; they watch and copy it. But then —wonderful Tudor irony! —

he has to scratch. In the end, when it looks as if he has prevailed, he too cannot escape physical distractions. Inner freedom and peace do not come so easily.

The structure of *Shadowplay* is very straightforward, very simple. And the movement Tudor has fashioned reflects all the shifts in mood and tension. Technically the ballet is not fiendishly difficult, but, as in all Tudor's work, the delicate relationship of the movement to the music — the demand for smooth transitions and control — is not exactly easy. One can very quickly lose contact with the dramatic tension. The atmosphere is created in two ways: first, the juxtaposition of the calm, fixed positions with the busier, more dramatic moments where there are large groups onstage; second, through the attitude, the *concentration*, of the dancer. You must keep a certain intensity working at all times.

I had worked with Tudor very little as I was getting the basic steps down and as he took the first rehearsals we had a very typical Tudor exchange. There's a place where the boy walks around picking up one foot and placing it either parallel to the other or at a certain strange angle. I had been taught these steps, but I found them a little puzzling. When I asked Tudor for help, he said, "Well, why are you doing it?" And I said, "Because these are the steps I was taught." And Tudor said, "Well, you never asked what it was all about. How could you possibly know how to do it?" And then proceeded to tell me, with utter authority and simplicity, that this passage is meant to reveal the boy's search for a proper place to meditate.

Shadowplay is the only Tudor ballet I have danced so far, and from it I learned a great deal about the kind of world, or at least about *one* kind of world, that interests him.

Shadowplay, it seems to me, is very much *about* Tudor. It is a work in which the parallels between the action as I have described it and the role of the artist in our society (an artist such as Tudor) are obvious. It is not difficult to imagine that *Shadowplay* reflects Tudor's need to concentrate in a special way, to see clearly before him what he must do. At the same time he is always remembering — and in his case, of course, with wit — the humanity and the fallibility of every man.

Le Spectre de la Rose

Choreography by Michel Fokine. Music by Carl Maria von Weber. Scenery and costumes by Leon Bakst. First performance by Diaghilev Ballets Russes, Monte Carlo, April 19, 1911, with Vaslav Nijinsky and Tamara Karsavina. First performance by Baryshnikov: Hamburg, September 22, 1975, with Lynn Seymour. Current American Ballet Theatre production (1941) staged by André Eglevsky. First performed by Baryshnikov (costume for **The Rose** by Stanley Simmons after Bakst), December 31, 1975, with Marianna Tcherkassky.

I had often seen *Spectre de la Rose* performed in the Soviet Union by such dancers as Yuri Soloviev of the Kirov and Maris Liepa of the Bolshoi. When I first danced it at the Nijinsky Gala in Hamburg, I was coached by André Eglevsky. (Lynn Seymour was taught the choreography — by mail! — by Margot Fonteyn.) Finally, I was very lucky that the American Ballet Theatre production was staged by Eglevsky, who admired the Fokine style tremendously and who remembered all the corrections Fokine had given him in private coaching sessions. This style is very easily recognizable, and yet very difficult to produce. Fokine's line is a special one, a kind of broken, soft harmony. It calls for the dancer to dance in a less stretched-out way, almost a little ``off.'' It's like playing with and reshaping the strict classical style.

*I*n dancing the part of The Rose, I have tried to deepen the ballet's dramatic implications even as I work to keep the specific Fokine style. *Le Spectre de la Rose* is almost a Freudian substitution: a rose for a man. The ballet deals with both the spiritual and erotic notions of ``roseness'': the essence of the rose. The Young Girl takes the rose from her breast (in those days, after all, only billets-doux were placed there), and it is quite clear that her mysterious vision is both ideally romantic and ideally erotic. It is important to communicate this balance between the spiritual and the sexual, but happily it is *there*, in the steps and in the style; the challenge lies in finding the full potential and the full balance.

The Rose is one of the most difficult roles I have ever danced. It is a marathon. When people think of *Le Spectre de la Rose* they think of one or two spectacularly executed leaps, or, as recent critics have noticed, many difficult and complicated turns. However, in the end — as in all Nijinsky roles — it is the legs that take the beating. The whole role is filled with plié, plié, *sissonne, sissonne*, without really taking off, or a combination of *sissonne, sissonne* into *entrechats-six, entrechats-six,* from and to a closed fifth position. Because I don't have a naturally short take-off, this kind of continual plié into big jumps makes it virtually impossible for me to get through the role. And in addition to all these technical difficulties there are also formidable stylistic complications — inseparable from the technique — to be considered. The dancer must flow, soften the standard classic arm positions, head positions, torso positions, to give the correct ``liquid'' modern Fokine configuration.

I enjoy dancing in *Le Spectre de la Rose* with its extraordinary atmosphere; its extraordinary perfume. But it does demand more than ordinary concentration, and a freedom of style that is difficult to achieve.

Le Pavillon d'Armide

Choreography by Michel Fokine. Music by Nicholas Tcherepnine. First performance: Maryinsky Theatre, Saint Petersburg, November 25, 1907, with Anna Pavlova, Paul Gerdt, and Vaslav Nijinsky. First performed (pas de quarte only) by Baryshnikov: Hamburg, September 22, 1975, with Zhandra Rodriguez, Marina Eglevsky, and Marianne Kruuse.

In the summer of 1975 I was invited by John Neumeier, the artistic director of the Hamburg Ballet, to appear in a special gala devoted to Nijinsky, dancing *Le Spectre de la Rose* and the famous *pas de quatre* from *Le Pavillon d'Armide.* Although I had never seen a full-length production of *Pavillon,* I was familiar with the Tcherepnine score and the variation from when I was in Russia. Alexandra Danilova taught me the steps; we performed the *pas de quatre* without traditional costumes as a simple and pleasant divertissement — a pretty little tableau.

The choreography — for three girls and a man — is typical of Fokine: sweet, moving, flowing. The male dancer supports each girl in turn as she dances a variation. Then there are four main variations and a coda. My own variation demonstrates something of what Nijinsky's dancing must have been like. The choreography calls for very big *sautés, entrechats-six* — all jumps from fifth position — and *échappés,* and is extremely hard on the legs. This Tcherepnine variation is very famous; it is still taught as a standard classical variation in the Soviet Union. It's very playful and delightful, if rather light. You can learn from it what Nijinsky must have had: extremely powerful legs. In the coda there is a very typical Fokine combination with *cabrioles écartées.* Big *écartés.* Fokine choreography often demands this of the male dancer — this very soft and difficult work for the legs.

It's a very odd sensation to dance a Nijinsky role. He was called ``king of the air'' because of his extraordinary *ballon*; many dancers have the kind of jump Nijinsky must have had, the kind of power in the legs that can produce many, many jumps from a closed position of the feet. Nijinsky must, in addition, have had a very strong Achilles tendon, which allowed for a short, fast take-off from a soft plié. I only performed the *Pavillon* variation once, but I would enjoy doing it again.

*A*s I have said, the prince is a much more active participant in the drama, he is not just a symbolic prop in the great metaphysical experience that is taking place. This becomes clearest in the last act, where, after he has fallen victim to the Black Queen's power, Bruhn's Siegfried dances a pas de deux with Odette that expresses the powerful nature of his relationship to her. It opens with Siegfried lying on the floor in despair; the Swan Queen lifts him and draws him up with the strength of her love. What follows is a duet of mutual understanding and forgiveness, as the choreography makes very clear. This pas de deux ends with Odette, exhausted, finally giving in. The struggle between the Black Queen and the prince continues, but even as Siegfried fights for Odette he is overcome by the storm magically created by the Black Queen. He dies, leaving the Swan Queen alone with her pain and the memory of her love. I think this is a very effective and powerful alternative ending to *Swan Lake.*

Technically this version of *Swan Lake* calls for a very accurate classical style; very strong, clear work. The adagio variation is lyrical and touching, very musical and expressive; the steps of this monologue or conversation with himself here somehow convey Siegfried's melancholia as well as a sense of premonition. The transitions into and out of the many arabesques in this variation are particularly well handled. Bruhn has choreographed the Black Swan pas de deux to different music, but I danced the standard, more familiar version.

THE ROYAL BALLET

Current Royal Ballet production (1971) choreographed by Nicholas Sergeyev after Petipa-Ivanov. Scenery and costumes by Leslie Hurry. First performed by Baryshnikov, London, October 27, 1975, with Merle Park.

The Royal Ballet's *Swan Lake* is a completely standard version of the great classic, and was not a particularly interesting experience for me from a dramatic point of view. It was, however, highly rewarding to work with the Royal Ballet and to begin to absorb another kind of style and attitude toward the classics. Michael Somes was extremely helpful in teaching me the "Royal" rhythm of walking and the rather deliberately heightened and stylized manner of partnering — English partnering — that fascinated me. He also helped me with the mime, which of course is very important in *Swan Lake,* and showed me how to maintain a constant "dryness" and clarity without looking deaf and dumb.

One of the things that preoccupied me in dancing the role of Siegfried in such a traditional version was the tension and dramatic level to be maintained during the two central pas de deux. When I was a little boy and we used to watch *Swan Lake* I would doze off and think, "Oh Lord, why isn't it over, won't it soon be over?" So now whenever I dance Siegfried it occurs to me that someone out in the audience may be thinking the very same thing. The public must be kept awake and in contact with the dancers throughout both these pas de deux, and in trying to achieve this it is very easy to make the whole atmosphere pretentious; to draw attention to oneself in a way completely at odds with the meaning and style of the ballet. Siegfried's idealistic love and wonderment in the second act, as well as his grand passion in the third, must be strong but kept within balance.

It is in a version such as this that the public and I become very aware of the possibilities and implications of partnering. Partnering has in fact changed very much for me since I came to the West. In the Soviet Union we were taught that it was of primary importance for the ballerina to be comfortable and secure; in the West these considerations are combined with greater attention to the male dancer's own sense of projection and line. Considerable advances have been made recently in the Soviet Union, however, many of them due to the influence of Vasiliev at the Bolshoi. Especially in the *Don Quixote* pas de deux he exhibited a male partnering style that could be considered revolutionary — his tauter, much more stretched outline and impact have begun to become important to the Russian male dancer. I have been very conscious of all these considerations and have worked extremely hard to develop my partnering style over the last few years.

Romeo and Juliet

Choreography by Kenneth MacMillan. Music by Serge Prokofiev. Scenery and costumes by Nicholas Georgiadis. First performance by the Royal Ballet, London, February 9, 1965, with Margot Fonteyn and Rudolf Nureyev. First performed by Baryshnikov, London, October 22, 1975, with Merle Park.

I had seen a private copy of the Fonteyn-Nureyev film of Kenneth MacMillan's *Romeo and Juliet* in the Soviet Union, as well as a privately made film of Antoinette Sibley and Anthony Dowell. I prepared Romeo for my London debut with Michael Somes, Donald MacLeary, Georgina Parkinson, and my Juliet, Merle Park.

In the Soviet Union the Lavrovsky version is sacred. It was originally created for Galina Ulanova and Konstantin Sergeyev, and has been imprinted with — and in fact confined by — their interpretations. The role of Romeo, for example, is still assigned to the most Sergeyev-like of the Kirov dancers, the most purely classical. Lavrovsky's ballet is extremely well constructed, very disciplined, clear, and restrained. But it is choreographically static. Kenneth MacMillan's adaptation allowed me to explore the role more freely. It is always important for me to figure out exactly how I can fit into an already extant ballet, and since so many people have danced Romeo successfully I had to think it through especially carefully in relationship both to the ballet and to Shakespeare's play. I am always looking for a fresh and original approach, not so much for the sake of originality, but so that I can be comfortable within the confines of a standard role. This *Romeo and Juliet* is primarily a story ballet. MacMillan has retained the major characters and the

basic situations, even though he does not retell the entire story A-B-C-D-E. He re-creates important, well-defined scenes, and evokes an atmosphere and emotions the viewer can relate to the great drama taking place before him. The central metaphor of his ballet is the pas de deux — the way in which the two young people come together and separate. And it is in these pas de deux that MacMillan has been most successful.

The characterizations are boldly conceived. When I began to rehearse the part of Romeo it seemed at first that I might have been more suited to Mercutio, but then I discovered that Romeo can be given a wide range of interpretations and offers enormous opportunities for artistic and dramatic growth. I had never thought of Romeo in a soft, romantic, or dreamy way — he was, for me, a very down-to-earth character. As I rehearsed, MacMillan often said, "You are too Mercutio, you are too naughty — be warmer and softer." What came out in the end was a hybrid. Romeo is, after all, a terribly impulsive and aggressive young man — the kind of guest the Capulets really should have thrown out of their ball. But underlying this rambunctiousness is a tender, passionate streak. His first meeting with Juliet is perhaps not cataclysmic, but she is a strange and fascinating girl to him and he is

intrigued in a way he has never been intrigued by any woman before. Then comes the balcony pas de deux — technically not impossible but very dizzying and difficult to control both on the level of dramatic and sexual tension and as sheer dance. Yet this scene must be less intense than the bedroom pas de deux, in which the young couple's passion springs forth full-blown, their physical and intellectual love reaching extraordinary heights.

MacMillan has devised many sensitive and well-constructed transitions in the dramatic schemes, and there are several particularly interesting developments within the characters themselves. The second-act market scene, with the death of Mercutio and the fight with Tybalt, is especially rewarding from this point of view. It is here that Romeo must reveal the transition from boyish ardor to mature love. In the beginning of the ballet, as in the beginning of love, Romeo does not really understand or know what his feelings toward Juliet are, or recognize that this love will eventually consume them. In the balcony duet we witness the beginning of the flame, but it is not entirely ignited, not fully blazing.

It is in the market scene, when Romeo receives the letter, that he is hit very hard, and in MacMillan's version the moment is emphasized. It is introduced by a charming comic episode with the nurse, which sets up a contrast to the heightened

feelings Romeo later experiences when he reads the letter, and which he must reveal to the audience. The scene with Tybalt then becomes very interesting to develop. It has traditionally been played by Romeo in a manner suggesting a kind of soft friendliness. It was my idea that Romeo display neither hostility nor any particular warmth toward Tybalt but recognize, pragmatically, that Tybalt is the favorite uncle, a man whose relationship to Juliet is a strong one. Romeo finds himself caught between two fools, Tybalt and Mercutio, and he doesn't want to take part in their silly argument; he proceeds, simply and straightforwardly, to try to placate Tybalt. In contrast to this direct and rational approach, the death of Mercutio comes as a terrible shock. Romeo becomes demented and hysterical, out of control, and suddenly senses that either he or Tybalt must die. In a daze he picks up the sword and begins automatically to fight. As he feels the cold steel,

reality takes over, and revenge becomes the most important thing in his mind. The duel is now a matter-of-fact execution. At the end of the scene, when he realizes how wild he has been and what the tragic consequences are to be, he bursts into tears like a child who has had a tantrum and behaved disgracefully.

Technically *Romeo and Juliet* is very rewarding to perform. The pas de deux are both creative and expressive, the steps musical and satisfying. It is very important that they be executed with great precision and simplicity, and with the maximum cleanness possible. Much of the choreography is extremely ``closed,'' filled with precise, small steps, very fast ronds de jambe, and quite exposed positions, such as *piqué* attitudes or *piqué* turns *à la seconde par terre.* It is not an enormously difficult role technically, but it is tiring—very *long*—and active dramatically throughout.

Awakening

Choreography by Robert Weiss. Music by Craig Steven Shuler. Costumes by Susan Tammany. First performance by American Ballet Theatre, New York, December 30, 1975, with Baryshnikov and Gelsey Kirkland.

Robert Weiss is the youngest choreographer I have ever worked with. In fact, this young choreographer, and young composer, and young designer, and Gelsey — well, I was the oldest of the lot. The musical score for this dance is sweet, like a bite of caramel candy. And that's very much the way the whole thing came out — an atmosphere of young love and trust, of innocent passion. This fresh and lyrical ballet was really a beginning — a good chance for Weiss to have two willing bodies working with him as he begins his career as a choreographer. We'll have to wait until his next piece to see where all these energies are going.

Hamlet Connotations

Choreography by John Neumeier. Music by Aaron Copland. Scenery by Robin Wagner. Costumes by Theoni V. Aldredge. First performance by American Ballet Theatre, New York, January 6, 1976, with Baryshnikov, Marcia Haydée, Gelsey Kirkland, Erik Bruhn, and William Carter.

John Neumeier had studied and loved Copland's *Connotations for Orchestra* for some time. He had long wanted to create a ballet to it but had abandoned the idea because it didn't seem to "work." American Ballet Theatre proposed, I believe, that he choreograph *Hamlet* to the famous score Shostakovich had composed for the film version; Neumeier then suggested his beloved Copland. He asked Copland for some additional music to fill out the score to the length required for the ballet as he envisioned it, Copland agreed, and they were off and running.

What particularly attracted Neumeier was the dramatic power of the score, and it was the idea of "connotations" which gave him his way of approaching *Hamlet* in dance terms. He never intended the ballet to be a literal translation of Shakespeare's play as did Konstantin Sergeyev in his very traditional Soviet production. Ballets such as Lavrovsky's *Romeo and Juliet* and John Cranko's

Eugene Onegin and *The Taming of the Shrew* are *illustrative* ballets; they provide a direct dance-narrative substitute for the text. But *Hamlet,* to begin with, is a more symbolic play, and Neumeier has chosen to abstract certain portions of the drama and re-create the symbolic conflict. The text of Shakespeare's play is a complicated mystery, but the action is very simple. This ballet extracts the emotional excitement, the tension, from Shakespeare's words and reinvests them in simple, symbolic actions. What John has done is create a dramatic world in which it is not the events of the story that are portrayed on the stage but the *reactions* to these events by the leading characters. In this ballet the action of the play takes place offstage; what you have in front of you is a kind of "scenes-we-never-saw" — an interior dramatization, as it were.

The construction of *Hamlet Connotations* is very complicated, but the movements reveal throughout a specific dramatic idea based on the play itself. For instance, when the ballet opens, the dancer who represents Hamlet's dead father is lying prone on the stage, blocking the entrance through which the dancers must come. There are individual solos for the four main characters, each of whom must step over the king's body in order to begin. All of them do this except Hamlet himself, who has not yet come to terms with the physical pain and memory of his father's death. Hamlet *cannot* step over his father's body. Gradually, with comparable symbolic touches, Neumeier reveals Gertrude's power and authority, Claudius's guilt and arrogance, Ophelia's madness, and Hamlet's famous but nonetheless very real indecision.

The steps of *Hamlet Connotations* are not extraordinarily difficult technically, despite the contractions and the breathing problems stemming from the many high jumps. But it is difficult to *perform*. It demands tremendous precision and control; the dancing is very exposed. And it is difficult to perform because I have to maintain a balance between the violence of much of the movement and an emotional control, and at the same time project a rapidly changing state of mind. All this while working on a very high-powered level.

The entire dance was choreographed in a style I was not completely familiar with, a kind of modern classical ballet. But Neumeier's intricate and highly developed theatrical ideas were very stimulating, and the music itself, with its warmth and emotional coloration, was always revealing and sustaining.

Push Comes to Shove

Choreography by Twyla Tharp. Music by Joseph Lamb and Franz Joseph Haydn. Costumes by Santo Loquasto. First performance by American Ballet Theatre, New York, January 9, 1976, with Baryshnikov, Martine van Hamel, Marianna Tcherkassky, and Clark Tippet.

When I first saw Twyla Tharp all I could think of was "You probably have to be born here to do it." This whole melange of classical ballet, jazz, tap, social dancing needs a special technique and a special accent that seemed so foreign to me. Strangely enough it was not the steps, not the movement, in Twyla Tharp's work that first attracted me, but her ideas about the music, her attitude toward music. I had seen the two works she had created for the Joffrey Ballet, *As Time Goes By* and *Deuce Coupe,* and was very struck by her personal understanding of music. It wasn't until I began to grasp how she worked musically that I could really concentrate on the "language" of the pieces. And as I began to understand and be able to take in that language, it was so unexpected and marvelous that I was swept off my feet. It was obvious to me from the beginning that her work was *serious,* and had a highly developed, *willed* style. Seeing her ballets opened up a whole new world of possibilities for the use of classical ballet steps.

I first met Twyla in Spoleto in 1975, where I had gone to dance John Butler's *Medea.* It was while watching Twyla perform her *The 100's* there that I saw how refined and delicate and impossibly difficult her vocabulary is. The most important thing about Twyla's work is that it is very controlled and classical in its intent. It never speculates and it's never arbitrary, and her demands in relationship to the music are more specific than almost anything I have ever done.

$\mathcal{A}$s I began to work with her I found things very difficult technically. The body movement is often slightly off balance — on purpose, of course — something completely foreign to my very straightforward, classical way of moving. There are many turns off balance, and there is a lot of off-balance work that demands a very strong demi-pointe and very strong ankles. All of this work in the legs and feet is played off against an extreme flexibility in the upper body. In Twyla's work the body can switch direction in the middle of the beat for any given movement. She not only has these changes in the arc of each movement, as well as complicated variations of them, but the choreographic structure is very broad, all over the stage, and performed at top speed. So the breathing is very difficult. As you are dancing you feel like a fish in the sand.

As I said, musically Twyla is extremely precise. We worked for hours and hours on the phrasing, which was very intricately developed. The flexibility of the body and the complexity of the movement parallels the flexibility of the phrasing — which also goes in and out, on and off the beat. When Twyla began working on *Push Comes to Shove* she created most of the movement for my main solo to a

piece by Bach, and after the music was changed to Haydn, most of the original movement was kept. Working on this solo was like going to the moon and back again, hours and hours and hours of very technical rehearsals, repetition over and over again. Twyla takes it for granted that the choreographer and the dancer can do a single *enchaînement* three thousand times to get it right. I had never had the habit or discipline to do anything so many times and with such concentration of energy. In classical ballet I more or less know what the possible is, but in this case I had no idea what I could or couldn't do. Twyla pushed me and encouraged me to accomplish many things I never would have dreamed I could do. She is a genius in the studio at keeping the energy level high and productive, and giving the dancers the moral strength to get to what she demands. I always had the feeling in the beginning that I was out in a boat that had no sail, doing forbidden things. She herself moves so beautifully, and there she was asking me to do it too. It was like a professional flautist saying to a professional pianist, "You're a musician; here, play this instrument the way I do." Except that while Twyla and I have basically the same instrument, my tone is not as beautiful as hers for *her* "music."

Push Comes to Shove is a tour de force. It's so meticulously constructed, so theatrically perfect. If you watch it carefully you see the seriousness of the piece, the seriousness of the intent. Many people say Twyla "gives them what they want." Well, she does. But her work also springs from complete dedication to an idea. In *Push,* for example, the balance is between two kinds of music. The rag with its jazzy upbeat rhythms is so skillfully attached to the Haydn that one can only think, well, yes, of course, that's the way it has to be. The opening section, which is set to the Joseph Lamb rag for Martine, Marianna, and myself — it's a calling card from Twyla to the audience: "This is where it all comes from, this is *my* tradition." That parentage is immediately established, an unpretentious, highly charged American-classical way of dancing. And then we move on to Haydn, but as we move from music that is Twyla's naturally to music that might not be, we see that her attitude toward the Haydn is as classical as the Haydn itself. She can work with it, push with it, play with it; she feels up to Haydn. The rhythmical structure of the dancing in the Haydn section is perhaps more developed and more complicated than anything I have known. Twyla's not afraid of the work, and attacks it, catches the fluidity and jazziness in the score. But she doesn't play with the music coyly. She takes it for what it is, and makes it into something logical and beautiful.

A lot of the work I first did in the West was new to me. But nothing was as new, as different, and, thank God, as inevitable as *Push Comes to Shove.* It's lovely that it was a big hit. But, more important, it was really new. For all of us.

Other Dances

Choreography by Jerome Robbins. Music by Frédéric Chopin. Costumes by Santo Loquasto. First performance: Gala Evening for the New York Public Library, May 9, 1976, with Baryshnikov and Natalia Makarova.

I think that when making *Dances at a Gathering*, Robbins had in the back of his mind additional music that would have been appropriate for that great ballet — but he never used it. *Other Dances* gave him the chance. He worked very quickly when we were preparing this pas de deux. He himself showed us everything; he moves beautifully, and could demonstrate very clearly the idiosyncratic changes, the shifts in direction he wanted. There is no *idea* for *Other Dances,* there is no story. Jerry talked to me through the music all the time. "Listen to the music," he would say, "listen to the music." "This is how I understand the music." And then he would show me one of those combinations that are so *his,* and so beautiful — the twists of the shoulder, the open, relaxed steps gradually changing into smaller, more delicate movements. We tried many versions of my solos. He "worked" the choreography very hard.

I think the most difficult thing for Jerry was to find the form — the structure — of the ballet. He approached each section as a musical whole, and then had to work out the sequence in a way that was theatrically sound. It is my feeling that the dances could have been placed in any order, even though the way it evolved resulted in what is very much a classical pas de deux structure: pas de deux, variations, variations, coda. He didn't use many verbal or psychological descriptions to elicit from us what he wanted. Sometimes he would say something as brief as, ``This is a military variation,'' or ``This pose is like a late nineteenth-century photograph; try and get that feeling.'' But basically the whole ballet is just a *musical idea.* It was born of and lives inside the music. Jerry understands it that way.

Technically *Other Dances* is quite difficult — even though very relaxed and harmonious — because it is so long for a pas de deux. And in certain ways it's harder to be relaxed onstage for that amount of time than to produce very high-powered technical virtuosities. The emotional tension of the piece is very calm and benign, and that, too, is difficult to maintain.

Working with Jerry was a complete revelation. Sometimes he would take a rehearsal and dance the whole thing for me; I wouldn't dance a step. But seeing him dance is what brought me closest to dancing it the way *he* wanted. He gave so much that I learned it all more quickly than I thought I would. He's stupendous!

"Pas de Duke"

Choreography by Alvin Ailey. Music by Duke Ellington. Scenery and costumes by Rouben Ter-Arutunian. First performance by Alvin Ailey City Center Dance Theatre, New York, May 11, 1976, with Baryshnikov and Judith Jamison.

When I first began working with Alvin Ailey on this new ballet all I could think of was that I looked like a cow on ice. Here I was with one of America's greatest dancers, Judith Jamison (I feel about her the way I feel about Fred Astaire), and I just didn't know what I was doing. I felt very ``complexed'' about the whole thing, very embarrassed.

And just the night before we began to rehearse, Alvin called and asked me to please not wear ballet slippers. I was to wear jazz shoes. That was the last straw. I thought, ``Oh, Alvin, give me one last chance, let me keep my dancing shoes!'' But of course he insisted.

``Don't look at me, don't look at me,'' I said at the first rehearsals. Then we began working to try to help me out of these difficulties a little. We started in the studio with Alvin, Judy, Alvin's assistant, and myself. Alvin would do Judy's part and the assistant would do my part, and for hours I would stand behind them copying the steps in my own clumsy fashion. All I could think of was ``This isn't dancing, what I'm doing, this is sheer klutz.'' Everyone paid compliments, but I didn't believe them.

What was difficult about it is obvious, I suppose. Here was a whole different world of movement. Not only the jazziness of it, but there were very difficult

contractions, real, full contractions that I found impossible to perform. And even more difficult than these were the lightning transitions from one step to another, the virtuoso kind of transitions which Alvin's dancers can make in their sleep. All I could think of was that being on stage with Judy was taking a big risk.

Naturally as time went on I became more familiar and more at ease with the steps. Alvin worked very closely with me. He would ask me to show him a kind of jump that he thought he wanted, and I would show him how it could be done classically, and then he would say, "Well, yes, do it, but do it going backwards, do it to the other side." It was very hard for me to coordinate the big classical jumps with the smaller, more accented jazz steps, but eventually it became more natural, and I felt less and less like a cow.

Even as the premiere came closer, I wasn't completely secure. Everyone kept encouraging and complimenting me, but I still didn't believe a word of it. I still felt, "I'm going to go out there and it's going to be as if I'd forgotten my dance belt. Somebody in the audience will stand up and scream 'You're naked! You're naked! What are you doing?'" But all through the rehearsal period I was watching Judy very carefully, seeing how her body worked and how Alvin used what she could do so beautifully. It sustained me.

When the performance came, nervous as I was, it was a thrill. It was great fun, really *fun* to dance, to have this kind of style developed on me to such a great piece of American music. I don't know whether I was satisfied with my work or not, but I did get through it. I hope Alvin was pleased with the results.

Petrouchka

Choreography by Michel Fokine. Music by Igor Stravinsky. Scenery and costumes by Alexandre Benois. First performance: Diaghilev Ballets Russes, Paris, June 13, 1911, with Vaslav Nijinsky, Tamara Karsavina, and Alexandre Orlov. Current American Ballet Theatre production (1942) first performed by Baryshnikov, New York, June 21, 1976, with Eleanor d'Antuono and Marcos Paredes; also danced with Karena Brock and Ted Kivitt.

I had never danced *Petrouchka* in the Soviet Union because it has not been a part of the standard classical repertory of the major companies there. A version was performed in the Maly Theatre in Leningrad, but it had undergone several radical choreographic changes over the years.

Petrouchka is a very mysterious and fascinating ballet — fascinating historically in what it reveals *about* Nijinsky and intriguing for what it must have meant *to* him. And at the same time it has its own endlessly provocative mysteries and contradictions. We know from Nijinsky's diaries, from such memoirs as those of Fokine and Benois, and especially from such recent distinguished critics as Vera Krassovskaya (whose book on Nijinsky, now being translated into English, I personally find fascinating) that the role of Petrouchka was critical to Nijinsky's whole career. The parallel between Petrouchka's situation and that of Nijinsky in his relationship to Diaghilev and the Diaghilev regime is quite clear. Krassovskaya points out that it was in the making and performing of this piece that many of Nijinsky's self-realizations became crystallized, and we can imagine that it was his perception of these parallels that elevated these performances to their legendary level.

Alexandre Benois has said that Nijinsky was a marionette in real life, a man with the simplest of internal mechanisms, but with an extraordinary sensitivity and the deepest of feelings which he covered with a primitive mask. One can easily appreciate how the story of *Petrouchka* — the triumph of the poetic spirit over the restraints of circumstance — must have held an extraordinary meaning for Nijinsky. Krassovskaya suggests that the role of Petrouchka was not deliberately and literally based on Nijinsky, but that various aspects of his behavior and his real life must have contributed unconsciously to the creation of this great masterpiece. Even many of his personal mannerisms were, so to speak, ideal for the part: very often, for instance, he was subject to mechanical gestures and tics, and would move as if confined in a small, enclosed room. Fokine obviously used these natural eccentricities to their fullest theatrical extent.

As a ballet, *Petrouchka* remains a perfectly fashioned puzzle, a complicated psychological — even political — drama. Structurally it is beautifully made. The opening section in which the three dolls are introduced is clearly a conventional, dramatic exposition. But in this exposition the whole drama that will afterwards unfold is already encapsulated. We know that Petrouchka is a trapped soul who is struggling to tear off his chains. Later, watching him in his cell, we realize that this struggle is a complicated one, a metaphysical one. Not only is he a puppet, trapped in his puppetness while his soul cries out to be human, but *as* a puppet he is victimized by the other puppets — the other *people* — around him. It is almost an existential drama.

Fokine has contrasted the opening fair scene and the two cell scenes almost cinematically. Scale is used as a camera would use a close-up, so that when we see Petrouchka in his cell we share in his drama as we share that of actors in the tightest close-up imaginable. The role of Petrouchka is not only a symbolic one; theatrically it has enormous range. The dancer must be able to project an extraordinary variety of feelings — joy, anger, pain, dejection, humiliation, triumph, glee — and characterize all these feelings in the manner of a straw doll. The challenge is almost insurmountable.

Krassovskaya compares Petrouchka to all the great heroes in Gogol, Dostoevsky, and Pushkin, and suggests why the role has become the role of the century — not only because of what it meant for and about Nijinsky, but because it reflected the growing interest and sensitivity of all artists to the freedom of the individual; that it is about small people being torn apart by fear and hate and humiliation, and their inevitable rebellion. It suggests how those feelings can finally emerge to control the destinies of the individual, no matter how primitive and deep the mask he hides behind may be.

The great irony, the tragedy, in this piece is revealed at the ballet's conclusion when Petrouchka who, theoretically, is a doll, dies. And yet you see his soul, or you see him *as* his soul, shouting his triumph, his freedom from the chains he has lived with, at the old magician who has been his cruel master. But when the magician leaves, Petrouchka collapses. The relationship between him and his hypnotic mentor is indissolvable. He cannot exist in freedom with him, but neither can he exist without him.

The writing on the doll's house in many productions says "Theatre of the Living." What is endlessly fascinating about this piece is that it is indeed a theatre of feelings, of psychological relationships, of political relationships — it is a whole world unto itself. A world of secrets that do not lock us out; of secrets that can nourish us forever.

Petrouchka is very difficult to perform, but it is hugely rewarding. It is difficult because the musical accents are very clear and the aural cues very accentuated. That is, the choreography, the steps, are often directly on the beat, and the steps and gestures come fast and furiously at a relentless pace, so that to stay on the music is a task in itself. The characterization is extremely clear, but difficult to make natural. The use of a puppetlike style must, first of all, be clearly designed and then performed with a seamless, fluid ease so that it becomes its own standard, so that the audience doesn't feel that the dancer is "playing a doll."

I have only danced *Petrouchka* twice, and I will need many performances before I feel comfortable with all the complexities that have to be dealt with in this role. But I love the ballet, and I love the role, and I will dance it.

Le Sacre du Printemps

Choreography by Glen Tetley. Music by Igor Stravinsky. Scenery and costumes by Nadine Baylis. First performance by the Munich State Opera Ballet, Munich, April 17, 1974, with Ferenc Barbay. First performance by American Ballet Theatre, New York, June 21, 1976, with Baryshnikov, Martine van Hamel, and Clark Tippet.

Any ballet version of *Le Sacre du Printemps* will be dominated by the dictates of Stravinsky's score. Tetley's solution is not, as others have been, a linear, literal interpretation of the Stravinsky libretto. Instead it is a series of impressionistic or symbolic scenes which relate very closely to Stravinsky's intent but not necessarily to each other, in one direct developmental line. It's almost impossible to speak about the music; so much has already been said. But I think its most important quality is that it is *not* dryly intellectual music. It is music about muscle and bone, sweat and sex. A very rich, primitive eroticism. The lead couple in *Le Sacre du Printemps* are very much a composite of these qualities, whereas the role I dance is more that of a kind of spiritual figure moving through a symbolic cycle of life.

This cycle is very clearly presented. The opening expresses the warmth of waking up, the sensual strength of stretching muscles; the burgeoning, elastic jumps end this first solo with a powerful sense of exultation, a readiness for spiritual as well as physical action. Soon after comes the sacrifice — a sacrifice that is very Christian in its iconography. This is followed by the second solo, which is deliberately different from the first and creates a kind of dramatic juxtaposition. In it, the male figure emerges reborn; his dance is very staccato; he moves like a young animal with great power and energy, with a *need* to move, but showing a certain lack of control, a lack of experience.

I was taught my role by Glen Tetley himself. He *talked* me through it — I didn't learn the ballet on counts, which is unusual with such complicated music. Glen is an extraordinary person to work for in the studio; extremely clear. He gave me enormous motivation. He exudes tremendous energy and high spirits, and has a very contagious manner, an excitement, which is critical in the studio when you're learning a new work.

He changed my part in *Sacre* slightly from its original incarnation; that is, he changed the plastique here and there, giving certain steps and combinations a different shape, one more appropriate to my body. And, in this extraordinarily difficult, physically complex, and exhausting ballet, he gave me a great sense of comfort and security.

The music, of course, is very sustaining in itself. It *is* dance music. It is full of strong, clear dance rhythms and the kind of magnetism and power that not only take over but support you as you perform. The ballet has no real story but the music is an invitation to drama. It is so strong that it creates its own difficulty; the technical complications of the role are made even more demanding as the music almost hypnotically pushes you to an extremely tense and high-powered energy level. It forces you to match its intensity.

Once More, Frank

Choreography by Twyla Tharp. Music (recorded by Frank Sinatra): "Something Stupid" by Carson C. Parks; "One for My Baby" by Harold Arlen and Johnny Mercer; "That's Life" by Dean Kay and Kelly Gordon. Costumes by Santo Loquasto. First performance by American Ballet Theatre, New York, July 12, 1976, with Baryshnikov and Twyla Tharp.

Twyla Tharp created *Once More, Frank* as a dance for herself and me for a special American Ballet Theatre gala performance. But it was more than just a *pièce d'occasion,* it was an enormously interesting experience. I was better prepared to work with Twyla than when she had made *Push Comes to Shove.* I had worked so carefully with her that the whole style and movement were much easier, and I was able to work more quickly and in a more concentrated fashion than before. But above and beyond this, making *Once More, Frank* held a peculiar professional interest for me. It was the first time I had ever worked in a situation where the choreographer was also dancing; sharing with Twyla the tension of making the piece and being in it at the same time. What was fascinating was to experience Twyla constantly changing from the authoritative figure the choreographer must be to the co-dancer whose psychological level was very much the same as mine.

*T*he dance itself is about American theatrical style. *Once More, Frank* was set to three Frank Sinatra songs I had known before — to me Frank Sinatra is one of the great American performers — but the songs are not in my blood the way they are in Twyla's. I believe it was Twyla's intent to reveal onstage her very personal feelings about these songs — their text, their music, and the whole theatrical tradition they came from. The dance was about Twyla and Mischa the dancers, working out a specific dance problem: How two dancers with such different backgrounds and styles and techniques can find a middle ground, a performing style that is sustaining to both of them.

    Once More, Frank was a controversial piece mostly because of the formal gala setting against which it was performed. But as a kind of experiment, and then just quite simply as two dancers alone with Frank Sinatra, it was a great pleasure for me.

DANCERS

All the photographs in this book are of Baryshnikov. Other principal artists who appear with him on the following pages are: